Branches in Bloom

Mary Grace van der Kroef

Copyright ©2023 Mary Grace van der Kroef
All Rights Reserved

Cover Art:
A watercolour painting:
Apple Blossoms Copyright ©2023 Mary Grace van der Kroef

Edited by: Kirsten Pamela McNeill (Worthy Writers Editing)

ISBN:
978-1-7777211-7-6 (ebook)
978-1-7777211-8-3 (paperback)

First Edition

Contents

Acknowledgments	III
Preface	V
Epigraph	VII
1. Spring	1
Pots of Hope	2
Green Spaces	4
Yesterday's Muck	6
Trickle	7
Thaw Collection	9
Sunday	10
Remember	12
Spring Sun	13
2. Summer	14
Brave Reflection	15

Beauty Adrip	17
Downpour	18
Water Lines	20
Forget Me Not	22
Living Liquid	23
Sacred Pact	25
3. Autumn	26
Summer Kiss	27
Walnut Greens	28
Storms of Orange	30
Autumn Overtaking	32
One Harvest Moon	34
Breeze a Lover	36
Maple Red	38
Fall Leaf Collection	40
Falling's Purpose	42
Second Dance	44
Autumn's Dignity	45
Autumn's Song	47

Leaf Litter	49
4. Winter	51
Dance of Frozen Rains	52
Morning Snow	54
Marching Frost	56
Winter's Whisper	58
First Snow Haiku	60
Snow Blanket	61
Walking With Snow Devils	62
December Night	64
Ice Waves	66
Green Remembering	67
5. Creatures	69
Amplified	70
Wriggle	72
Hummingbird of Green	74
Raptor King	76
Mourning Love	78
Invading Cloud	80

Winged Day Shadow	82
Red Winged Knight	85
A Breath for a Sparrow	87
King of Blue	89
Arachnid Artist	91
6. Moments	93
Mountain Glory	94
Rain Soaked	95
Under	96
Nature's War	97
Rock Sentinel	99
Stone Murals	99
Air	99
Storm	99
About the Author	99

Acknowledgments

Pots of Hope was originally published in Dwelling Literary's GREENHOUSE Issue on May 21st, 2021 (Page 22)

Walnut Green and **Falling Purpose** both first appeared in Issue 23 Summer 2022 of Door is a Jar Magazine.

Preface

My northern upbringing has been a great source of inspiration for this collection and it pulls from poems I wrote between 2018 and 2023. You may find a fair amount of frost creeping into Spring and Autumn. I've also been told I use the words 'leaves' and too much. But I'll be honest with you, I didn't have the heart to edit out as many references to them as I should have. I've always loved trees, and was born in Autumn, married in Autumn, and birthed my first child under its changing hues. Please forgive their overuse. I pray at least a touch of my love for them shows through the pages of this book.

Thank you for taking the time to step into my mind and heart by reading the verses collected here. May they bless and uplift your spirit no matter what season or moment they find you in.

Mary Grace van der Kroef

"The heavens declare the glory of God,
and the sky above proclaims his handiwork."

- Psalms 19:1 ESV Holy Bible -

Spring

Pots of Hope

---

have you heard
plastic pull as the knife slides
across bags of black earth?

have you felt
beginnings of warmth as matter clings to
fingerprints
stains nails dark?

the dirt is chill
yet warmth flows
packed in pots of hope

have you listened
to the rustle of paper release seeds
from captivity?

smallness
containing miraculous promises

now may linger
but add a pane of glass to a sun of spring
and greenhouses blossom

It makes my heart sing

Simple actions reminding
surrounded by soil's grounding scent

Green Spaces

Boxed in green spaces
Scatterings of grass
come alive at winter's pass

Receding snow
revealing browns
sleeping beneath

Is waking a relief?

Or could you sleep
beneath spring
only listening

Come alive
drinking light

In the thaw there's fight
a waking right

Underneath the boots of man
crushed
in mixing mass

Green spaces enduring
to last

Yesterday's Muck

Rain
wet earth
are the scents
of new birth

Yester's leaves
brown
black
Composting piles
aromas unpack

Uncovered decay
warming
sunlight
Mid yesterday's muck
Spring made right

Trickle

Might
within a trickle
that crawls across my path

Rolling by
reflections
carry pieces of a past

Following the low path
down
ever on

Dissipating tendrils
hurry
comes the sun

Finding every crevice
every crack, a canyon wall

Losing molecules
seeping through pavement's claw

Reaching for haven
in iron rusted brown

Piling union
rising
to fall and drown

Trickles
come calling
perseverance goes beyond

Small revelations
strength
life's liquid throng

Thaw Collection

i

Once perfect white hill
strap particles in spring thaw
Speckled remnants glare

ii

Sweat from sun's new heat
Chilled while shade is guarding
Canada's spring sings

iii

Muddied crystals strewn
rippled ground tormented mix
Soon the soak will drain

Sunday

(Sabbath)

The passing winter mourned
as busyness begins
Remember friend, despite the sun
rushing never wins
Still there's need for peace
yet a need for rest
Take the day God gifted you
he knows what man needs best

Reach for the bud
the blossom that unfurls
Step on the warming green
releasing toes to curl
Invite a friend or two

to gather and agree
As the Holy Spirit greets
the fellowship of thee

The Sabbath for his people
His spring for spreading life
Don't let the need to DO and GO
introduce you to their strife
Take His pause for peace
drinking in your fill
Of fresh and new and sun-kissed dew
His command for rest, fulfill

Remember

How long has it been
since I bared my feet to earth and grass
felt the tickling kiss of living things?

How long has it been since
the cold dew wet my skin
and muddied my footprints?

Am I now old?
Time has spun and I forgot
that dirt was a fine plaything

Peel off Time's crusted pain
feel the earth again
Is it possible to remember?

Spring Sun

Out in a sun
That seed dreams
Heating metal armrests
Too a fierce burn
Soil, to a warm glow
That nurtures newness

Come rains to drizzle
On garden beds
Softening shells of shyness
Allowing anchors to break through
And fasten self
To reality
We awaken alongside
The saplings and perennials
Ready

Summer

Brave Reflection

When the sun knocks upon the earth
At summer's birth
It wakes bravery as a reflection

Watch it grow with hearty stocks that reach
Toward promise
Stretching roots deep in soured earth

Spreading green fronds
A shade for parched soil
Unafraid to grow a second span if plucked

Aggressive yellow waving toward the one
That woke them
Bursting blooms faded to wispy white

Spread sunshine with a breath
Coating grass in misunderstood love that
Children gather to place in water glasses

Bouquet withered in a day
Still, some of us remember woven crowns
That marked our heads as royal

They are looked for
Though their nourishment is forgotten while we
Manicure our lawns

Banish them to sidewalk cracks
Neglected ditches
They still shine back warmth that woke them

Beauty Adrip

Beauty adrip like
Slowly spun sugar crystals
Honeysuckle kiss

Downpour

Silent warning
lightning flash
all is quiet
Sudden *crash*

If only one
had looked up high
seen the ribbons in the sky

Now rain it pours
drenching crown
wave on wave
pummels ground

Unprepared
and keen alike

nature pours
a rattling strike

Some men scurry
to batten down
while others seem
content to drown

Hardships
For one and all
Nature has no favourites
It rains on all

Water Lines

I walked the line
Half a slosh with sucking sands
Sticking
attention commands
Yet on the left
a burn
For waves of liquid relief
yearn

So close they touch
as waves encroach the shore
I retreat
from kisses sweet
to again walk the line

Unable to break the need
for both

Forget Me Not

I'm sure they weren't there before
But here, they burst
A bunch of blue so new it laughs as I look on
Tiny joys
Deceptively dainty
As they laugh their way into flower beds
Unbidden
I don't have the heart
To stop encroaching blooms
So they become a blanket that cries for all to
Forget-Me-Not

Living Liquid

Accepted with an embrace
As waves give way to footsteps
Parting
With an easy flow
Settling around paused ankles
Toes

So different
Yet made of the same
Human matter
Living liquid

To stand at the edge
Of a body so vast...
And think, "You know me,"
As wisdom is shared through touch

A bit of me departs
Drops of it stay
Welcomed
By pours to swim
Through veins

Salty saturation
Is shed with a wave
Do I hear it whisper
"Come again?"

Sacred Pact

As sunlight kisses water
It leaves a residue
Of iridescent mirth

Read the love held
In shifting glimpses
Untold worth
As water meets the warming air

Human vision wavers
For this, a private act
Earth and sun pull shimmers
Veiling their devotion
The sacred pact

Autumn

Summer Kiss

Summer
Kiss the earth goodbye
Light her love with fire's blush
As she waves each leaf
With cheer
Promise her another year

(2021, October 3rd Chippewa Falls driving north to Fort Frances.)

Walnut Greens

Heavy with green
spheres

Weighted
to bend low

Shake a branch
release
gather
baskets brimming full

Blessed by heaviness in
buckets

Time
to shell the walnuts

*(Remembering Grandpa John
and his walnut trees.)*

Storms of Orange

Orange haze
nature's rage
pressures meet
on Sky's stage

Torrents fall
releasing gusts
thunder shouts
electric thrusts

Soaked through
rushing on
shelter found
liaison

The storm speaks
words felt
with every drop
nature pelts

In control
she flaunts it all
brushing past
humanity's gall

Storms of orange
fade to grey
nature's flirt
can truly slay

Autumn Overtaking

Starting with the crowning leaves
it trickles down with slow intent
Until all burn with crimson glow
A constant wave, hours, days old

Watch the tree be kissed by fire
Red, yellows, lingering greens
Ombre waves, a colour tide
How long until it all consumes?

Converts each leaf as colours flirt
and flit, and drip, and turn
Not alone, it kisses all
each a different hue

Fire transformed to gold
as light skips from maple to aspen
From sugar to quaking
autumn overtaking

One Harvest Moon

It's 5:30 am

Mr. Moon is peering through my window

Wearing his harvest glow like a luminous gem

Pulling the clouds around himself like a soft collar

Starting to dip beyond the trees topmost branches

Casting limbs and lingering leaves into silhouette

It's 6 am

The tiny child at my side sleeps

October's chill Shielded by our shared blanket

Mr. Moon don't wake her again

It's 6:30 am

The sky is deepest navy blue

Mr. Moon, your framing glow is dipping low

It's almost time to say goodnight

My day starts with a sleepy blur

I can almost hear a murmured purr

"Goodnight little Mother."

How can I be upset?

Dressed in his best, he's lonely

It's 6:45 am.

Navy turns to dusky blue

I've almost lost his golden view

His exit brings frosty fog that creeps and crawls

7:00 am

Sky now misty purple

How I wish he'd come again

Breeze a Lover

The breeze, a lover

Tugging on a partner's hand

A gentle dance to lead

The leaf, a partner

Flitting in artful embrace

Fragile yet holding strength

I, a hidden spy

From windows dark I peer

Glimpsing love beyond my years

Tree, a father

From seed to sapling now a king

Watching children court

Nature, a mother

Lends a blessing to her child

Wandering to find a place

I, a wisp in time

Privileged to glimpse the dance

Breeze and his romance

Falling, dance is done

Giving in to love

Fly her high, a butterfly, falling dance undone

Maple Red

See new blush upon the leaves
Slowly spread
Deepening as it flows
To maple's deepest red

Perhaps we humans stole these shades
For moments
Soft and close
o paint cheeks as we embrace

A tribute to nature's love
That deepens woody roots
While releasing laughter's leaves
Nourishment through winter's silence

The first sign of this acceptance
This dance that nodes at death
The evidence of time's ministrations
As he flirts with nature's chilling breath

Fall Leaf Collection

I

Foliage falling
Released from life forlorn
To feed hungry earth

ii

Leaf of brown crumbling
Dried and crackling crunching frail
Feeling the first snow

iii

Dead dry and helpless
Catches cold lacy crystals
A cup of passage

iv

Encrusted with cold
Dead leaves become gems
Frost sarcophagus

Falling's Purpose

Rustling like paper
Something not quite right

Curling edges
Unlucky sail
Or maybe...

A tumbling tail

Scrapes of character
Notches of wisdom
Travelling over pavement sealed

It wears, edges disintegrating
As journey works its sandpaper sadness

Remains
Sad threads the ghosts of waving life
Rest in gutters
Adding to the soupy slush

Fallen foliage found its end...

Or newness
as drain drinks these memories of trees

Taking essence
Down rivers to quench nature's thirst

Second Dance

Morning rush, drive fast
A cyclone follows closely
Memories dance twice

Autumn's Dignity

While the leaves are falling
and the wind is growing chill
God's hand is in this dying
though his actions aren't for ill

Turning gold and crimson
frost paints crystal fingerprints
across His canvas of colours
revealing glory's hints

Majestic change, an apogee
in array, autumns evening gown
God ends the season's spectacle
no modesty to be found

So death we see her dignity
One must lapse for more to begin
And that which ends, lives on in us
Lending life to guest and kin

Lord, I see your loving hand
Cradle all within your thoughts
When my autumn draws in close
may I end, as You allot

Autumn's Song

Listen to the crowning leaves
their glory days proceed with ease

The wind it gives to them a voice
they shout, with shaking blades rejoice

First time snow has run away
autumn has another day

Hands of gold shimmering shine
their dying days a heavenly shrine

With every wave a chorus raise
together singing turning's praise

Not to weep as down they fall
forming royal carpets for all

Soon their sheen will dull and brown
but in the cries there is no frown

It's well known they've earned this rest
The richest crown marks them as blessed

The first time snow has come and gone
so autumn plays us one last song

Leaf Litter

Leaves of memories
discarded in their time
no longer making nourishment
no longer being kind

How a tree is
wise when it lets them fall
upon roots to melt away
silence, rustles call

Naked through harsh winter
there's no need to cling
a past that doesn't feed
to truth that lost its ring

Roots will use the litter
as blanket holds back cold
then turn it into wisdom
that in spring unfolds

Winter

Dance of Frozen Rains

They're falling
tiny bits of white
This beating heart accepting it
as right

Swirling
on winds of winter's change
It's a dance
of frozen rains

Not a single shard
freezes quite the same
As lace with personality
holds its own name

Can you read them
before they melt away?
From fingertips warm
only a second display

Morning Snow

It may be dark inside
but without its growing light
As the world lay sleeping
nature donned a blanket white

Though the sky is thick
with heavy clouds of grey
Early morning darkness
is lightened by winter's play

I sit in my dark room
watching nature's lights return
Black to grey, then blue and white
the seasons complete a turn

Off in the distance
past trees and lake, there's more
Under clouds horizon peeks
a glimmer over the far shore

It was white and bright but brief
as if the sun is shy
It's been a while since winter played
beneath a sun-filled sky

So she'll stay behind her clouds
soften down her light
This first encounter not the time
she'll savour her delight

Marching Frost

It's painting a story across my window
not with strokes
but it creeps
The linking crystals
creak

Can you hear the chinking
Freezing water drops
first sheathed
then penetrated, cold
Crystallized armour
seconds old

Slow marching magic
materializing
by nature's written rule

Condensation pools
An opening for frost's
invading jewels

Camaraderie
found in moments of
shifting
chilling glass
I stand watching tiny
triumphs pass

Winter's Whisper

Winter whispers, "I'm coming home."

Crystals crackling cold
creeping across moist surfaces

Winter whispers, "I"m almost there."

Withering winds whip
wandering leaves to turmoil

Winter whispers, "I won't be long."

Lingering lullabies lilt longingly
as wings fly south

Winter whispers, "Wait for me."

Expectant eyes enamoured by elegance
watch white flakes fall

Winter whispers, "Are you ready?"

Drifts drape landscapes in a demure gown
when Winter comes to call

First Snow Haiku

---

i

Frozen crystals fall
Soft togetherness, blankets
Footprints, slow pools form

ii

Heavy snow falling
Youthful exuberance shines
Beneath the grey sky

iii

Come to me winter
Welcome to your birthing day
Now comes earnest play

Snow Blanket

A blanket of cold
Gentle, as it floats from deep
Enclosed sky. Now sleep

God-given layers
cover nature's dying throws
Dignity at end

Disintegrating
a slow giving up of self
powder feeds the earth

Walking With Snow Devils

(Snow tornado)

The air is crisp
stings my face
Earth is dressed
in snowing grace

As I walk
the sun gleams
on icy roads
in glistening beams

Deceptive warmth
despite the cold
Beckoning
to walk the road

While from my back
wind lifts
loosened snow
from growing drifts

In the air
flight becomes dance
spirals up
twisting advance

So like a ghost
spirit in flight
the wind cries out
a moment's fright

I freeze in place
watch it cease
Moment in time
my world at peace

Then in one breath
wind pulls anew
and I must question
if I saw true

Spied I a devil
in the wind?
Have nature's dreams
and reality twinned?

December Night

Mantle of lights above my head
fixed on a map of midnight blue
shining silver azure and red
so close, yet eons overhead

These only wink with my own blink
a steady stream of glistening
shining bright, yet light, I see
is all ancient history

A vastness more than mind can hold
yet I behold December's night
stand on my globe of living rock
that spins with the celestial clock

Count the numbers, multiply
as the universe flies by
here I stand a single speck
in heaven's sum

December night, clear, bright
gifted glimpse of creations might
never a doubt in my mind
stargazing, meant to remind

Ice Waves

Crystal air
Can you breathe?
Hanging low
Over water's soul
Free moving, heaving
Transforming
Sculpted glass ridges
Sharp
Refracting light
Through gates piled high
Growing through waves
Towards sky

Green Remembering

I smelled fresh cut grass
in the middle of February
While the wind was blowing fast
the clouds heavy

The smell was green
moist
lush
I inhaled it
as snow began to rush

Blowing clouds of white
obscuring my view
Somehow I still sniffed summer
far away

Like smoke
on the winds of memories

Behind my eye of glass
safe from the storm
I'm pulled
towards a dream that grieves
for spring

Memories seem old
withered pages of a book
silent movie tracks
faded photo's placed behind smudged screens

Still, I breathed in green
as brightness against the black and white scene
Remembering

Creatures

Amplified

Lilting notes
never heard so true

Captured
in wobbled tunes
that have carried me through months in
Winter's cocoon

Raising choirs
from December to June
Different feathers
they work together

Silent
humanity sits in fear

While birds sing of hope
despite uncertainty so near

(*Written during pandemic lock down 2021*)

Wriggle

(Gypsy Moth)

Wriggle
It creeps upon the leaf
tiny furry creature
eat at peace

Then appears a second
A third
to crunch and munch
Soon a hoard of creepers
Dispatching contented lunch

Once a glowing beauty
Now stripped
of gilded filigree

while they
weave wreathing nests
across a naked frame

Living drips
Her ravaged beauty
Proclaimed

Waiting through the darkness
Chrysalis of change
Until upon her skeleton
wings they all display

Watch
the ravenous darlings
Don gowns of chestnut
trimmed
with greying fur
Rising up they crown her new
their harvest now
conquered

Hummingbird of Green

(Ruby-Throated Hummingbird)

Hummingbird of green
Ruby-Throated sheen
The glimmer of your hue
Beauty that is true

Do you hear the hum?
Do you see them come?
Darting here and there
Flitting everywhere

Figure eight in flight
Flashing feathers bright
Tantalizing hover
Then darting off for cover

Tiny glory beam
A mesmerizing scene
Living dancing jewel
Fed by nature's fuel

Bill, uniquely devised
Giving access to the prize
Nectar that is sweet
Truly artistry complete

You bring a spirit here
That makes it crystal clear
Without you, nature we be
Achingly less free

Raptor King

(The Bald Eagle)

Feathered glory
Talons tight
Wingspan stretched
Ready for flight

As you lift
Towards the sky
A piercing call
Declares you're nigh

Using winds
Heights to soar
Gliding close
To lake and shore

The eagle master
Of the sky
No need to ask
The rhyme of why

As gliding over
Waves of blue
You show your skill
As hunter true

When silver sleek
Hangs from your feet
Few would dare
With you compete

Enjoy the catch
This feast will bring
It was well caught
Our Raptor King

Mourning Love

(Mourning Dove)

He seeks his lady fair
Will she make a pair?

Hear his wooing coo
Calling out for you

The safety of his perch
With earnestness his search

He wears the softest brown
Highlights pink and blue his crown

She chooses carefully
Believing in her artistry

Weaves a bed of love
Soft as a velvet glove

To hold their clutch of two
Cover them from view

They sit together well
Despite any storms that swell

-

Together love as one
Until their brood has run

With milk their squabs they raise
Within their infant phase

When the season's done
Goodbye to summer sun

Come again next spring
Together on the wing

Invading Cloud

(European Starling)

A cloud that moves with magic flight
Its span speaks of numbers might
The ringing of their call is bright
Wakes the world to view the sight

Murmurations on the wing
A waltz designed to praises bring
They rule sky, together sing
Flying close then part in stings

Comes the Starling unafraid
To every mile they have strayed
Conquered the land in a cascade
A tide we could not evade

In sheens of purple and of blue
Speckles white, like silver dew
Their grandeur we cannot subdue
A beauty we could never shoo

Twas our mistake to let them spread
This land was not their creation bed
But now to it they are well wed
On its bounty, they're well fed

So hear the Starling call with pride
Have no need to run and hide
Their persistence cannot be denied
Now to man, how they are tied

Winged Day Shadow

(The Raven)

You, a feathered
Trickster king
Strategist of
Stone and string

Dishevelled though
Your cloak may seem
Your eyes with
Intelligence gleam

Your silhouette
A striking size
Graceful shapes
Across the skies

Soaring higher
Not afraid
Resilience
Is your crusade

A shadow during
Brightest day
That frolics in
The winds at play

Many hear your
Call with fear
Understanding
Remains unclear

Man married you to
Death most foul
Through human dreams
We let you prowl

Yet fascinated
By your cackle
Curious
At its strange crackle

Truly you are
More a blend
A loyal treasure
Giving friend

If one can win
Your attention

With patience
Gentle affection

Send your ire
Not my way
I wont believe
The lies they say

There is no evil
In your flight
Honest respect
Is now your right

Red Winged Knight

(Red Winged Blackbird)

This marsh is where you've grown
Amid the reeds, you make a throne
Wearing a cloak of night
Highlighting shoulders bright
They flash a vivid red
By them love is led

Your mate demure in brown
striped is her gown
A mother through and through
To her clutch alone she's true
Weaves a basket nest
Industry her motherly zest

A "Chit chit chit," floats
Answering your silver notes
Hear a song of shrill intent?
On defence it's bent
A knight in crimson ash
Not afraid to clash

His own he will protect
Demanding all respect
Red Winged Bird in black
I'll heed your swift attack
Admire from afar
Thankful to know who you are

A Breath for a Sparrow

As the sparrow rests
Supported
By a life-giving friend
Who bears its weight
Fills its lungs
With life
It raises a song
That I drink in

I pass it
To the foliage
That hungers for my release
Of breath
So we all blend
While wandering

I
A sparrow
This aged tree
We three are free
Yet tethered together by need
Of each other

If the elder had eyes
To watch my departing steps
Would it wave a wind
To pillow my back
In competition with its friend
That flits ahead
Down my path?
Or do roots
Still feel my tread upon their back?

Securing my way
Sparrow heralds a humans presence
With gasps that ring
With life
So I turn and exhale
leaving a gift for both

King of Blue

(Blue Jay)

In the early morning grey
I see you
In the trees that shed their leaves
I see you
King of Birds of Blue

You're a brightness in the morn
Clouds are filling up with scorn
As bits of white fall
You're the brightest blink of all

Heaviness is falling down
Let it fall
Building on the weathered posts

Let it fall
You're still king through it all

Painted by the shifting light
magnificent through winter's white
Unafraid to face the chill
that amplifies your royal thrill

Don't fly away my King of blue
I'll look for you
For frozen months remain
I'll look for you
Jay, my morning view

Arachnid Artist

Silken strands strung stunningly
a woven web of artistry
Secretions from innovation's soul
yet born to place each strand
just so

Elegant economic pattern
drops of diamond dew bespattered
Stops one dead in tracks this morn
Now to face arachnid
scorn

To such a masterpiece destroy
A humble apology employ
Hours spent on spinning threads

a masterpiece of newness
spreads

Moments

Mountain Glory

The glory of a mountain peak
Is like a friend who doesn't speak

Light that plays on glassy lake
Almost moves a heart to break

But if it breaks this pain is kind
It only serves us to remind

There are many friends
Beyond mankind

Rain Soaked

Drops swelling by degrees
pummelled
deep within me
Drenching soul same as dress
showers filled with blessedness

Bedraggled though I may appear
I will not censure
honest cheer
for reservation is a snare
when such rains are rare

Under

Trembles only felt
Never seen by world at large
Have given roots strength

Nature's War

Street lights
cast
a shimmering glow
as sheets of rain
pass
row on row

Drops
hit pavement
scattering dance
A fight with earth
Or
nature's romance

Water escapes
into each tiny crack

Eroding
man's hold
turning
time back

From pavement
to sand
the battle is slow
But nature has
timed
its endless flow

Rock Sentinel

Gawking eyes
read your lines
in drive-by waves
from metal mines

Bare a soul
ripped wide
So metal mines
can drive straight lines

Stone Murals

Sharp edges
multicoloured pores
showing off scars
human endeavours

Broken stones
We've blasted wide
Essence laid bare
in cascading lines

Revealing a mural
history vast
Our earth bleeds colours
down lesions that last

Air

The strength to carry life across a planet rift with strife
The will to feed a multitude of lungs
with self
Hoarding nothing of held wealth

To give, spread, be stolen away
A single indrawn breath
Exhaled rest

Is the breeze through my window

Storm

Lightning strikes
Follow thunder's sound
Rain in sheets that
Pound the ground

Stops a heart
Cold in its tracks
View the clouds
Built in stacks

Trapped in awe
At this storm's rage
Watch the dance
Across sky's stage

Blinks could miss
The last farewell
As winds push past
The show to quell

About the Author

Mary Grace van der Kroef is a poet, writer, and artist from Ontario, Canada. She enjoys the simple things in life, like a good cup of coffee and heart-to-heart talks with friends. She uses her writing to highlight those simple things while encouraging others and exploring her own inner world. She is a follower of Jesus Christ and writes from a Christian worldview. She believes every person, regardless of circumstance, is a creative being whose stories are important. She cherishes people's differences and believes diverse stories are imperative to understanding what it is to be human.

Website: www.marygracewriting.ca
Subscribe to Mary Grace's monthly newsletter by visiting her website and filling out the form on the home page. The newsletter lets you enjoy a monthly update from Mary on her writing and her family life. Subscribing also ensures that you are notified of any special sales of Mary's art or books. Stay in touch and up-to-date by subscribing today!

Twitter: @MGWriting

Instagram: @mrygracewriting

Facebook: @marygracewriting

Shop Mary's various art prints and products at Mary's Redbubble Shop:

https://www.redbubble.com/people/MaryGWriting/shop

www.ingramcontent.com/pod-product-compliance
Lightning Source LLC
Chambersburg PA
CBHW042128100526
44587CB00026B/4211